CW00519060

Deliciously Pescatarian

Achieve a Healthy Way of Life with
Easy Fish and Seafood Recipes

Jacob Aiello

© copyright 2021 – all rights reserved.

the content contained within this book may not be reproduced, duplicated or transmitted without direct written permission from the author or the publisher.

under no circumstances will any blame or legal responsibility be held against the publisher, or author, for any damages, reparation, or monetary loss due to the information contained within this book. either directly or indirectly.

legal notice:

this book is copyright protected. this book is only for personal use. you cannot amend, distribute, sell, use, quote or paraphrase any part, or the content within this book, without the consent of the author or publisher.

disclaimer notice:

please note the information contained within this document is for educational and entertainment purposes only. all effort has been executed to present accurate, up to date, and reliable, complete information. no warranties of any kind are declared or implied. readers acknowledge that the author is not engaging in the rendering of legal, financial, medical or professional advice. the content within this book has been derived from various sources. please consult a licensed professional before attempting any techniques outlined in this book.

by reading this document, the reader agrees that under no circumstances is the author responsible for any losses, direct or indirect, which are incurred as a result of the use of information contained within this document, including, but not limited to, — errors, omissions, or inaccuracies.

Table of Contents

Salt and Pepper Shrimp

Servings: 4

Total Time: 30 Minutes

Calories: 228

Fat: 8.9 g

Protein: 26.4 g

Carbs: 9.3 g

Ingredients and Quantity

- 2 tsp. peppercorns
- 1 tsp. salt
- 1 tsp. sugar
- 1 lb. shrimp
- 3 tbsp. rice flour
- 2 tbsp. oil

Direction

1. Set the Ninja Foodi to sauté.

2. Roast the peppercorns for 1 minute and then allow them cool.

3. Crush the peppercorns and add the salt and sugar.

4. Coat the shrimp with this mixture and then with flour.

5. Sprinkle oil on the Ninja Foodi basket.

6. Place the shrimp on top.

7. Cook at 350 degrees for 10 minutes, flipping halfway through.

8. You can serve with fresh salad. Enjoy!

Tuna Patties

Servings: 2

Total Time: 45 Minutes

Calories: 141

Fat: 6.4 g

Protein: 17 g

Carbs: 5.2 g

Ingredients and Quantity

- 2 cans tuna flakes
- 1/2 tbsp. almond flour
- 1 tsp. dried dill
- 1 tbsp. vegan mayo
- 1/2 tsp. onion powder
- tsp. garlic powder
- Salt and pepper, to taste
- 1 tbsp. lemon juice

Direction

1. Mix all the ingredients in a bowl and then form patties.

2. Set the tuna patties on the Ninja Foodi basket.

3. Seal the crisping lid.

4. Set it to air crisp.

5. Cook at 400 degrees for 10 minutes.

6. Flip and cook for 5 more minutes.

7. You can serve with fresh green salad. Enjoy!

Lemon Garlic Shrimp

Servings: 4

Total Time: 50 Minutes

Calories: 170

Fat: 5.5 g

Protein: 26.1 g

Carbs: 2.8 g

Ingredients and Quantity

- 1 lb. shrimp, peeled and deveined
- 1 tbsp. olive oil
- 4 garlic cloves, minced
- 1 tbsp. lemon juice
- Salt, to taste

Direction

1. Mix the olive oil, salt, lemon juice and garlic.

2. Toss shrimp in the mixture.

3. Marinate for 15 minutes.

4. Place the shrimp in the Ninja Foodi basket.

5. Seal the crisping lid.

6. Select the air crisp setting.

7. Cook at 350 degrees for 8 minutes.

8. Flip and cook for 2 more minutes.

9. You can sprinkle chopped parsley on top. Enjoy!

Tasty Steamed Lobster Tails

Servings: 4

Total Time: 15 Minutes

Calories: 353

Fat: 24.5 g

Protein: 32.2 g

Carbs: 0.9 g

Ingredients and Quantity

- Four 6 oz. lobster tails
- Salt and pepper, to taste
- 1/2 cup butter

Direction

1. Place the Ninja Foodi reversible rack inside the
   ceramic pot.

2. Pour a cup of water in the pot.

3. Season the lobster tails with salt and pepper to taste.

4. Place the seasoned lobster tails on the reversible rack.

5. Close the pressure lid and set the vent to SEAL.

6. Press the Steam button and adjust cooking time to 10 minutes.

7. Do quick pressure release.

8. Once the lid is open, take the lobster tail out and serve with butter on top.

Spicy Steamed Shrimps

Servings: 2

Total Time: 12 Minutes

Calories: 360

Fat: 4.4 g

Protein: 41.1 g

Carbs: 38.8 g

Ingredients and Quantity

- 1 pound tiger prawns with shell
- 1 packet Old Bay seasoning
- 1 jar cocktail sauce

Direction

1. Place the Ninja Foodi Cook and Crisp reversible rack inside the ceramic pot.

2. Pour a cup of water in the pot.

3. Season the prawns with Old Bay seasoning.

4. Place the shrimps on the reversible rack.

5. Close the pressure lid and set the vent to SEAL.

6. Press the Steam button and adjust the cooking time to 10 minutes.

7. Do quick pressure release.

8. Serve with cocktail sauce. Enjoy!

Walleye Pickerel with Butter and Lemon

Servings: 8

Total Time: 24 Minutes

Calories: 336

Fat: 15.6 g

Protein: 43.9 g

Carbs: 4.8 g

Ingredients and Quantity

- 8 fillets walleye pickerel

- 1/4 cup almond butter
- 1/4 cup lemon juice
- 1 large onion, sliced into rings
- Salt and pepper, to taste

Direction

1. Place the Foodi Cook and Crisp reversible rack inside the ceramic pot.

2. Pour a cup of water in the pot.

3. On a large aluminum foil, place the pickerel and pour over the almond butter, lemon juice, salt and pepper.

4. Garnish with onion rings on top.

5. Close the aluminum foil and crimp the edges.

6. Place on the reversible rack.

7. Close the pressure lid and set the vent to Seal.

8. Press the Steam button and adjust the cooking time to 20 minutes. Serve and enjoy!

Steamed Tilapia and Veggies

Servings: 6

Total Time: 18 Minutes

Calories: 134

Fat: 2.4 g

Protein: 23.6 g

Carbs: 4.4 g

Ingredients and Quantity

- 1 tsp. olive oil
- 6 tilapia fillets
- 1 pinch Greek seasoning
- 4 stalks celery, halved
- 1 cup fresh baby carrots
- 1 bell pepper, cut into chunks
- 1/2 onion, sliced
- Salt and pepper, to taste

Direction

1. Place the Foodi Cook and Crisp reversible rack inside the ceramic pot.

2. Pour water into the pot.

3. Brush oil on to the tilapia fillets.

4. Season with Greek seasoning, salt and pepper.

5. Place the tilapia fillets on the basket.

6. Layer the veggies on top.

7. Close the pressure lid and set the vent to Seal.

8. Press the Steam button and adjust the cooking time to 15 minutes. Serve and enjoy!

Tasty Steamed Fish

Servings: 6

Total Time: 18 Minutes

Calories: 137

Fat: 1.1 g

Protein: 29.7 g

Carbs: 1.9 g

Ingredients and Quantity

- 6 halibut fillets
- 1 tbsp. dried dill weed
- 1 tbsp. onion powder
- 2 tsp. dried parsley
- 1/4 tsp. paprika
- 1 pinch salt
- 1 pinch lemon pepper
- 1 pinch garlic powder
- 2 tbsp. lemon juice

Direction

1. Place the Ninja Foodi Cook and Crisp reversible rack inside the ceramic pot.

2. Pour water into the pot.

3. Season the halibut fillets with dill weed, onion powder, dried parsley, paprika, salt, pepper, garlic powder, and lemon juice.

4. Place the seasoned fish fillets on the reversible rack.

5. Close the pressure lid and set the vent to SEAL.

6. Press the Steam button and adjust the cooking time to 15 minutes. Serve and enjoy!

Chinese Style Steamed Garlic Prawn

Servings: 10

Total Time: 25 Minutes

Calories: 67

Fat: 1.8 g

Protein: 12.1 g

Carbs: 1.8 g

Ingredients and Quantity

- 20 large tiger prawns, shells not removed
- 2 tbsp. soy sauce
- 5 garlic cloves, minced
- 1 tbsp. brandy

Direction

1. Place all ingredients in a Ziploc bag and marinate in the fridge for at least 2 hours.

2. Place the Foodi Cook and Crisp reversible rack inside the ceramic pot.

3. Pour water into the pot.

4. Place the marinated shrimps on the reversible rack.

5. Close the pressure lid and set the vent to SEAL.

6. Press the Steam button and adjust the cooking time to 20 minutes. Serve and enjoy!

Steamed Lemon Grass Crab Legs

Servings: 4

Total Time: 30 Minutes

Calories: 564

Fat: 20.7 g

Protein: 89.1 g

Carbs: 5.3 g

Ingredients and Quantity

- 2 tbsp. vegetable oil

- 3 garlic cloves, minced
- 1 piece fresh ginger root, crushed
- 1 stalk lemon grass, crushed
- 2 tbsp. fish sauce
- 1 tbsp. oyster sauce
- 2 pounds frozen Alaskan king crab
- Salt and pepper, to taste

Direction

1. Place the Foodi Cook and Crisp reversible rack inside the ceramic pot.

2. Pour water into the pot.

3. Combine all ingredients in a big Ziploc bag and marinate for at least 30 minutes.

4. Place the crabs on the reversible rack.

5. Close the pressure lid and set the vent to Seal.

6. Press the Steam button and adjust the cooking time to 25 minutes. Serve and enjoy!

Healthy Egg Bites

Preparation Time: 10 minutes

Cooking Time: 13 minutes

Serve: 4

Nutritional Value (Amount per Serving):

- Calories 125
- Fat 8.1 g
- Carbohydrates 2.8 g
- Sugar 2.1 g
- Protein 9.8 g
- Cholesterol 178 mg

Ingredients:

- 4 eggs, lightly beaten
- ¼ cup cheddar cheese, shredded
- ½ cup bell pepper, diced
- ½ cup almond milk

- ¼ tsp garlic powder
- Pepper
- Salt

Directions:

1. Preheat the air fryer to 325 F.

2. Add all ingredients into the bowl and whisk until we combined.

3. Spray silicone muffin molds with cooking spray.

4. Pour egg mixture into the silicone muffin mold and place it in the air fryer basket and cook for 8-10 minutes.

5. Serve and enjoy.

Easy Potato Wedges

Preparation Time: 10 minutes

Cooking Time: 10 minutes

Serve: 6

Nutritional Value (Amount per Serving):

- Calories 174
- Fat 8.6 g
- Carbohydrates 23.8 g
- Sugar 1.7 g
- Protein 2.5 g
- Cholesterol 0 mg

Ingredients:

- 2 lbs potatoes, cut into wedges
- 2 tbsp chipotle seasoning
- ¼ cup olive oil

- Pepper
- Salt

Directions:

1. Add potato wedges into the bowl.

2. Add remaining ingredients over potato wedges and toss well.

3. Transfer potato wedges into the air fryer basket and cook for 10 minutes. Turn potato wedges halfway through.

4. Serve and enjoy.

Sweet Potatoes & Brussels Sprouts

Preparation Time: 10 minutes

Cooking Time: 20 minutes

Serve: 4

Nutritional Value (Amount per Serving):

- Calories 135
- Fat 7.4 g
- Carbohydrates 17.2 g
- Sugar 3.9 g

- Protein 4.4 g
- Cholesterol 0 mg

Ingredients:

- 2 sweet potatoes, wash, and cut into 1-inch pieces
- 1 lb Brussels sprouts, cut in half
- ¼ tsp chili powder
- 2 tbsp olive oil
- ¼ tsp garlic powder
- ½ tsp pepper
- 1 tsp salt

Directions:

1. Preheat the air fryer to 400 F.

2. Add sweet potatoes, Brussels sprouts, and remaining ingredients into the bowl and toss until well coated.

3. Transfer sweet potatoes and Brussels sprouts mixture into the air fryer basket and cook for 20 minutes. Stir halfway through.

4. Serve and enjoy.

Healthy Spinach Frittata

Preparation Time: 10 minutes

Cooking Time: 8 minutes

Serve: 1

Nutritional Value (Amount per Serving):

- Calories 190
- Fat 11.7 g
- Carbohydrates 4.3 g
- Sugar 3.3 g
- Protein 15.7 g
- Cholesterol 337 mg

Ingredients:

- 2 eggs, lightly beaten
- ¼ cup spinach, chopped
- ¼ cup tomatoes, chopped
- 2 tbsp almond milk

- ¼ tsp garlic powder
- 1 tbsp parmesan cheese, grated
- Pepper
- Salt

Directions:

1. In a bowl, whisk eggs. Add remaining ingredients and whisk until well combined.

2. Spray small air fryer pan with cooking spray.

3. Pour egg mixture into the prepared pan.

4. Place pan into the air fryer basket and cook at 330 F for 8 minutes.

5. Serve and enjoy.

Breakfast Potatoes

Preparation Time: 10 minutes

Cooking Time: 20 minutes

Serve: 6

Nutritional Value (Amount per Serving):

- Calories 105
- Fat 2.5 g
- Carbohydrates 18.5 g
- Sugar 1.5 g
- Protein 2.1 g
- Cholesterol 0 mg

Ingredients:

- 1 ½ lbs potatoes, diced into ½-inch cubes
- ¼ tsp chili powder
- ¼ tsp pepper
- 1 tsp paprika

- 1 tsp garlic powder
- 1 tbsp olive oil
- Salt

Directions:

1. Add potatoes and remaining ingredients into the bowl and toss well.

2. Add potatoes into the air fryer basket and cook at 400 F for 20 minutes. Stir potatoes halfway through.

3. Serve and enjoy.

Spinach Pepper Egg Bites

Preparation Time: 10 minutes

Cooking Time: 20 minutes

Serve: 6

Nutritional Value (Amount per Serving):

- Calories 60
- Fat 4.2 g
- Carbohydrates 1.7 g
- Sugar 1.1 g
- Protein 4.1 g
- Cholesterol 109 mg

Ingredients:

- 4 eggs
- 1/2 cup spinach, chopped
- 1/2 cup roasted peppers, chopped
- 1/8 cup almond milk

- 2 tbsp green onion, chopped
- 1/4 tsp salt

Directions:

1. Preheat the air fryer to 325 F.

2. In a bowl, whisk eggs with milk and salt. Add spinach, green onion, and peppers and stir to combine.

3. Pour egg mixture into the silicone muffin molds.

4. Place muffin molds into the air fryer basket and cook for 12-15 minutes.

5. Serve and enjoy.

Egg Cheese Muffins

Preparation Time: 10 minutes

Cooking Time: 20 minutes

Serve: 6

Nutritional Value (Amount per Serving):

- Calories 165
- Fat 13.7 g
- Carbohydrates 1.4 g
- Sugar 0.4 g
- Protein 8.9 g
- Cholesterol 151 mg

ngredients:

- 4 eggs
- 1 scoop whey protein powder
- 2 tbsp butter, melted
- 4 oz cream cheese
- Pepper
- Salt

Directions:

1. Preheat the air fryer to 325 F.

2. Add all ingredients into the bowl and whisk until combine.

3. Pour batter into the silicone muffin molds.

4. Place muffin molds into the air fryer basket and cook for 20 minutes.

5. Serve and enjoy.

Mushroom Spinach Muffins

Preparation Time: 10 minutes

Cooking Time: 15 minutes

Serve: 6

Nutritional Value (Amount per Serving):

- Calories 75
- Fat 5 g
- Carbohydrates 0.9 g
- Sugar 0.5 g
- Protein 6.1 g
- Cholesterol 140 mg

Ingredients:

- 5 eggs
- 1 cup spinach, chopped
- 1/4 tsp onion powder
- 1/2 cup mushrooms, chopped

- 1/4 tsp garlic powder
- Pepper
- Salt

Directions:

1. Preheat the air fryer to 375 F.

2. In a bowl, whisk eggs with garlic powder, onion powder, pepper, and salt. Add spinach and mushrooms and stir well.

3. Pour egg mixture into the 6 silicone muffin molds.

4. Place muffin molds into the air fryer basket and cook for 10-12 minutes.

5. Serve and enjoy.

Egg Veggie Soufflé

Preparation Time: 10 minutes

Cooking Time: 20 minutes

Serve: 4

Ingredients:

- 4 eggs
- 1/2 cup mushrooms, chopped
- 1 tsp onion powder
- 1 tsp garlic powder

- 1/2 cup broccoli florets, chopped
- Pepper
- Salt

Nutritional Value (Amount per Serving):

- Calories 85
- Fat 5.1 g
- Carbohydrates 2.4 g
- Sugar 1.1 g
- Protein 7.1 g
- Cholesterol 186 mg

Directions:

1. Preheat the air fryer to 350 F.
2. Spray four ramekins with cooking spray and set aside.
3. In a bowl, whisk eggs with onion powder, garlic powder, pepper, and salt. Add mushrooms and broccoli and stir well.
4. Pour egg mixture into the prepared ramekins.

5. Place ramekins into the air fryer basket and cook for 20 minutes.

6. Serve and enjoy.

Italian Egg Muffins

Preparation Time: 10 minutes

Cooking Time: 20 minutes

Serve: 12

Nutritional Value (Amount per Serving):

- Calories 65
- Fat 4.4 g
- Carbohydrates 2.1 g
- Sugar 1.2 g
- Protein 4 g
- Cholesterol 87 mg

Ingredients:

- 6 eggs
- 3 cherry tomatoes, chopped
- 4 sun-dried tomatoes, chopped
- 1/2 cup feta cheese, crumbled

- 2 tsp olive oil
- Pepper
- Salt

Directions:

1. Preheat the air fryer to 350 F.

2. In a bowl, whisk eggs with pepper and salt. Add remaining ingredients and stir well.

3. Pour egg mixture into the 12 silicone muffin molds.

4. Place half muffin molds into the air fryer basket and cook for 12-15 minutes.

5. Serve and enjoy.

Marinated Ginger Garlic Salmon

Preparation Time: 10 minutes

Cooking Time: 10 minutes

Serve: 2

Nutritional Value (Amount per Serving):

- Calories 334
- Fat 18.2 g
- Carbohydrates 9 g
- Sugar 3.4 g
- Protein 35.7 g
- Cholesterol 78 mg

Ingredients:

- 2 salmon fillets, skinless & boneless
- 1 1/2 tbsp mirin
- 1 1/2 tbsp soy sauce
- 1 tbsp olive oil
- 2 tbsp green onion, minced
- 1 tbsp ginger, grated
- 1 tsp garlic, minced

Directions:

1. Add mirin, soy sauce, oil, green onion, ginger, and garlic into the zip-lock bag and mix well.

2. Add fish fillets into the bag, seal the bag, and place in the refrigerator for 30 minutes.

3. Preheat the air fryer to 360 F.

4. Spray air fryer basket with cooking spray.

5. Place marinated salmon fillets into the air fryer basket and cook for 10 minutes.

6. Serve and enjoy.

Chili Honey Salmon

Preparation Time: 10 minutes

Cooking Time: 12 minutes

Serve: 2

Nutritional Value (Amount per Serving):

- Calories 336
- Fat 11.2 g
- Carbohydrates 26.8 g
- Sugar 26 g
- Protein 34.8 g
- Cholesterol 78 mg

Ingredients:

- 2 salmon fillets
- 3 tbsp honey
- 1/2 tbsp chili flakes
- 1/2 tsp chili powder

- 1/2 tsp turmeric
- 1 tsp ground coriander
- 1/8 tsp pepper
- 1/8 tsp salt

Directions:

1. Add honey to microwave-safe bowl and heat for 10 seconds.

2. Add chili flakes, chili powder, turmeric, coriander, pepper, and salt into the honey and mix well.

3. Brush salmon fillets with honey mixture.

4. Place salmon fillets into the air fryer basket and cook at 400 F for 12 minutes.

5. Serve and enjoy.

Tender & Juicy Honey Glazed Salmon

Preparation Time: 10 minutes

Cooking Time: 10 minutes

Serve: 4

Nutritional Value (Amount per Serving):

- Calories 271
- Fat 13.1 g
- Carbohydrates 4.5 g
- Sugar 4.3 g

- Protein 34.7 g
- Cholesterol 78 mg

Ingredients:

- 4 salmon fillets
- 1 tbsp honey
- 1/2 tsp red chili flakes, crushed
- 1 tsp sesame seeds, toasted
- 1 1/2 tsp olive oil
- 1 tbsp coconut aminos
- Pepper
- Salt

Direction

1. Place salmon fillets into the bowl. In a small bowl, mix coconut aminos, oil, pepper, and salt and pour over fish fillets. Mix well.

2. Cover bowl and place in the refrigerator for 20 minutes.

3. Preheat the air fryer to 400 F.

4. Place marinated salmon fillets into the air fryer basket and cook for 8 minutes.

5. Brush fish fillets with honey and sprinkle with chili flakes and sesame seeds and cook for 2 minutes more.

6. Serve and enjoy.

Easy Herbed Salmon

Preparation Time: 10 minutes

Cooking Time: 5 minutes

Serve: 2

Nutritional Value (Amount per Serving):

- Calories 407
- Fat 30.8 g
- Carbohydrates 0.2 g
- Sugar 0 g
- Protein 34.6 g
- Cholesterol 94 mg

Ingredients:

- 2 salmon fillets
- 1 tbsp butter
- 2 tbsp olive oil
- 1/4 tsp paprika

- 1 tsp herb de Provence
- Pepper
- Salt

Directions:

1. Brush salmon fillets with oil and sprinkle with paprika, herb de Provence, pepper, and salt.

2. Place salmon fillets into the air fryer basket and cook at 390 F for 5 minutes.

3. Melt butter in a pan and pour over cooked salmon fillets.

4. Serve and enjoy.

Lemon Butter Salmon

Preparation Time: 10 minutes

Cooking Time: 12 minutes

Serve: 2

Nutritional Value (Amount per Serving):

- Calories 344
- Fat 22.6 g
- Carbohydrates 1.1 g
- Sugar 0.3 g
- Protein 35 g
- Cholesterol 109 mg

Ingredients:

- 2 salmon fillets
- 1/2 tsp soy sauce
- 3/4 tsp dill, chopped
- 1 tsp garlic, minced

- 1 1/2 tbsp fresh lemon juice
- 2 tbsp butter, melted
- Pepper
- Salt

Directions:

1. Preheat the air fryer to 400 F.

2. In a small bowl, mix butter, lemon juice, garlic, dill, soy sauce, pepper, and salt.

3. Brush salmon fillets with butter mixture and place into the air fryer basket and cook for 10-12 minutes.

4. Pour the remaining butter mixture over cooked salmon fillets and serve.

Perfect Parmesan Salmon

Preparation Time: 10 minutes

Cooking Time: 10 minutes

Serve: 4

Nutritional Value (Amount per Serving):

- Calories 294
- Fat 16 g
- Carbohydrates 3.7 g
- Sugar 1 g
- Protein 34.8 g
- Cholesterol 82 mg

Ingredients:

- 4 salmon fillets
- 1/4 cup parmesan cheese, shredded
- 1/4 tsp dried dill
- 1/2 tbsp Dijon mustard

- 4 tbsp mayonnaise
- 1 lemon juice
- Pepper
- Salt

Directions:

1. In a small bowl, mix cheese, dill, mustard, mayonnaise, lemon juice, pepper, and salt.

2. Place salmon fillets into the air fryer basket and brush with cheese mixture.

3. Cook salmon fillets at 400 F for 10 minutes.

4. Serve and enjoy.

Quick & Easy Salmon

Preparation Time: 10 minutes

Cooking Time: 8 minutes

Serve: 4

Nutritional Value (Amount per Serving):

- Calories 269
- Fat 14.5 g
- Carbohydrates 0.7 g
- Sugar 0.2 g
- Protein 34.7 g
- Cholesterol 78 mg

Ingredients:

- 4 salmon fillets
- 1/2 tsp smoked paprika
- 1 tsp garlic powder
- 1 tbsp olive oil

- Pepper
- Salt

Directions:

1. Preheat the air fryer to 400 F.

2. Brush salmon fillets with oil and sprinkle with smoked paprika, garlic powder, pepper, and salt.

3. Place salmon fillets into the air fryer basket and cook for 8 minutes.

4. Serve and enjoy.

Healthy Salmon Patties

Preparation Time: 10 minutes

Cooking Time: 8 minutes

Serve: 6

Nutritional Value (Amount per Serving):

- Calories 105
- Fat 4.8 g
- Carbohydrates 0.7 g
- Sugar 0.2 g
- Protein 14.2 g
- Cholesterol 64 mg

Ingredients:

- 1 egg
- 1 tsp paprika
- 2 green onions, minced
- 2 tbsp fresh coriander, chopped

- 14 oz can salmon, drain & mince
- Pepper
- Salt

Directions:

1. Preheat the air fryer to 360 F.

2. Add all ingredients into the bowl and mix until well combined.

3. Spray air fryer basket with cooking spray.

4. Make the equal shape of patties from the mixture and place into the air fryer basket and cook for 8 minutes.

5. Serve and enjoy.

Flavorful Salmon Fillets

Preparation Time: 10 minutes

Cooking Time: 10 minutes

Serve: 2

Nutritional Value (Amount per Serving):

- Calories 366
- Fat 25.4 g
- Carbohydrates 1.5 g
- Sugar 0.6 g
- Protein 35 g
- Cholesterol 78 mg

Ingredients:

- 2 salmon fillets, boneless
- 1/2 tsp garlic powder
- 1/2 tsp ground cumin
- 1/2 tsp chili powder

- 2 tbsp fresh lemon juice
- 2 tbsp olive oil
- Pepper
- Salt

Directions:

1. In a small bowl, mix oil, lemon juice, chili powder, ground cumin, garlic powder, pepper, and salt.

2. Brush salmon fillets with oil mixture and place into the air fryer basket and cook at 400 F for 10 minutes.

3. Serve and enjoy.

Basil Cheese Salmon

Preparation Time: 10 minutes

Cooking Time: 7 minutes

Serve: 4

Nutritional Value (Amount per Serving):

- Calories 414
- Fat 22.4 g
- Carbohydrates 1.8 g
- Sugar 0.5 g
- Protein 46.6 g
- Cholesterol 110 mg

Ingredients:

- 4 salmon fillets
- 1/4 cup parmesan cheese, grated
- 5 fresh basil leaves, minced
- 2 tbsp mayonnaise

- 1/2 lemon juice
- Pepper
- Salt

Directions:

1. Preheat the air fryer to 400 F.

2. Brush salmon fillets with lemon juice and season with pepper and salt.

3. In a small bowl, mix mayonnaise, basil, and cheese.

4. Spray air fryer basket with cooking spray.

5. Place salmon fillets into the air fryer basket and brush with mayonnaise mixture and cook for 7 minutes.

6. Serve and enjoy.

Sriracha Salmon

Preparation Time: 10 minutes

Cooking Time: 12 minutes

Serve: 4

Ingredients:

- 1 lb salmon fillets
- 1 tbsp soy sauce
- 1/2 cup honey
- 4 tbsp sriracha

Nutritional Value (Amount per Serving):

- Calories 296
- Fat 7 g
- Carbohydrates 38.2 g
- Sugar 34.9 g
- Protein 22.4 g
- Cholesterol 50 mg

Directions:

1. In a bowl, mix soy sauce, honey, and sriracha. Add fish fillets and mix well, cover and place in the refrigerator for 30 minutes.
2. Spray air fryer basket with cooking spray.
3. Place marinated salmon fillets into the air fryer basket and cook at 400 F for 12 minutes.
4. Serve and enjoy.

Garlic Brown Sugar Salmon

Preparation Time: 10 minutes

Cooking Time: 10 minutes

Serve: 4

Ingredients:

- 1 lb salmon fillets
- 3/4 tsp garlic powder
- 1 tsp Italian seasoning
- 1/2 tsp smoked paprika
- 3/4 tsp chili powder
- 2 tbsp brown sugar
- Pepper
- Salt

Nutritional Value (Amount per Serving):

- Calories 175
- Fat 7.5 g

- Carbohydrates 5.4 g
- Sugar 4.7 g
- Protein 22.2 g
- Cholesterol 51 mg

Directions:

1. In a small bowl, mix garlic powder, Italian seasoning, paprika, chili powder, brown sugar, pepper, and salt and rub over salmon fillets.

2. Spray air fryer basket with cooking spray.

3. Place salmon fillets into the air fryer basket and cook at 400 F for 10 minutes.

4. Serve and enjoy.

Blackened Salmon

Preparation Time: 10 minutes

Cooking Time: 7 minutes

Serve: 4

Nutritional Value (Amount per Serving):

Calories 274

Fat 14.8 g

Carbohydrates 1.7 g

Sugar 0.3 g

Protein 34.9 g

Cholesterol 78 mg

Ingredients:

- 4 salmon fillets
- 3/4 tsp dried thyme
- 3/4 tsp dried oregano
- 1/2 tsp garlic powder
- 1/2 tsp cayenne
- 1 tbsp sweet paprika
- 1 tbsp olive oil
- Pepper
- Salt

Directions:

1. Preheat the air fryer to 400 F.

2. In a small bowl, mix thyme, oregano, garlic powder, cayenne, paprika, pepper, and salt.

3. Brush salmon fillets with oil and coat with spice and herb mixture.

4. Place salmon fillets into the air fryer basket and cook for 7 minutes.

5. Serve and enjoy.

Honey Mustard Salmon

Preparation Time: 10 minutes

Cooking Time: 10 minutes

Serve: 2

Nutritional Value (Amount per Serving):

- Calories 296
- Fat 13.8 g
- Carbohydrates 9.7 g
- Sugar 8.8 g
- Protein 35.1 g
- Cholesterol 78 mg

Ingredients:

- 2 salmon fillets
- 1 tsp paprika
- 1 tsp olive oil
- 1 tbsp Dijon mustard

- 1 tbsp honey
- Pepper
- Salt

Directions:

1. Preheat the air fryer to 400 F.

2. In a small bowl, mix honey, mustard, oil, paprika, pepper, and salt.

3. Brush salmon fillets with honey mixture and place into the air fryer basket and cook for 10 minutes.

4. Serve and enjoy.

Chili Sauce Salmon

Preparation Time: 10 minutes

Cooking Time: 15 minutes

Serve: 2

Nutritional Value (Amount per Serving):

- Calories 541
- Fat 33.6 g
- Carbohydrates 16.3 g
- Sugar 3.8 g
- Protein 44.5 g
- Cholesterol 115 mg

Ingredients:

- 1 lb salmon fillets
- 1 1/2 tbsp sriracha
- 1/3 cup Thai chili sauce
- 1/2 cup mayonnaise

- Pepper
- Salt

Directions:

1. In a small bowl, mix sriracha, chili sauce, mayonnaise, pepper, and salt.
2. Brush salmon fillets with sriracha mixture and place into the air fryer basket and cook at 400 F for 13-15 minutes.
3. Serve and enjoy.

Easy Cod Fillet

Preparation Time: 10 minutes

Cooking Time: 10 minutes

Serve: 1

Nutritional Value (Amount per Serving):

- Calories 72
- Fat 0.4 g
- Carbohydrates 1 g
- Sugar 0.3 g
- Protein 16.9 g
- Cholesterol 27 mg

Ingredients:

- 3 oz cod fillet
- 1/8 tsp garlic powder
- 1 lemon slice

- Pepper
- Salt

Directions:

1. Season cod fillet with garlic powder, pepper, and salt.

2. Place cod fillet into the air fryer basket and top with a lemon slice.

3. Cook cod fillet at 375 F for 10 minutes.

4. Serve and enjoy.

Lemon Dill Cod

Preparation Time: 10 minutes

Cooking Time: 10 minutes

Serve: 4

Nutritional Value (Amount per Serving):

Calories 204

Fat 12.3 g

Carbohydrates 1.4 g

Sugar 0.2 g

Protein 21.2 g

Cholesterol 73 mg

Ingredients:

- 4 cod fillets
- 1 tsp dried dill
- 2 tbsp lemon juice
- 1 1/2 tbsp garlic, minced
- 1/4 cup butter, melted
- Pepper
- Salt

Directions:

1. Preheat the air fryer to 370 F.

2. In a bowl, mix butter, garlic, lemon juice, dill, pepper, and salt. Add cod fillets and coat well.

3. Place fish fillets into the air fryer basket and cook for 10 minutes.

4. Serve and enjoy.

Quick Chili Lime Cod

Preparation Time: 10 minutes

Cooking Time: 10 minutes

Serve: 2

Nutritional Value (Amount per Serving):

Calories 159

Fat 8.3 g

Carbohydrates 1.7 g

Sugar 0.3 g

Protein 20.4 g

Cholesterol 40 mg

Ingredients:

- 2 cod fillets
- 1 tbsp olive oil

- 1/4 tsp ground cumin
- 1/2 tsp garlic powder
- 1/2 tsp chili powder
- 1/2 tsp dried oregano
- 1 tsp dried parsley
- 3/4 tsp smoked paprika
- 1 lime zest, grated
- Salt

Directions:

1. Add oil, cumin, garlic powder, chili powder, oregano, parsley, paprika, and salt into the zip-lock bag and mix well.

2. Add cod fillets into the zip-lock bag, seal bag, and place in the refrigerator for 30 minutes.

3. Preheat the air fryer to 380 F.

4. Place marinated fish fillets into the air fryer basket and cook for 10 minutes.

5. Serve and enjoy.

Parmesan Cod Fillets

Preparation Time: 10 minutes

Cooking Time: 7 minutes

Serve: 2

Nutritional Value (Amount per Serving):

Calories 619

Fat 34.6 g

Carbohydrates 19.5 g

Sugar 1.7 g

Protein 47.6 g

Cholesterol 115 mg

Ingredients:

- 2 cod fillets
- 1/4 cup parmesan cheese, grated

- 1/2 cup whole-wheat breadcrumbs
- 1/4 tsp Italian seasoning
- 2 tbsp olive oil
- Pepper
- Salt

Directions:

1. In a shallow dish, mix parmesan cheese, breadcrumbs, Italian seasoning, pepper, and salt.
2. Brush fish fillets with oil and coat with cheese mixture.
3. Place fish fillets into the air fryer basket and cook at 390 F for 7 minutes.
4. Serve and enjoy.

Miso Sea Bass Fillets

Preparation Time: 10 minutes

Cooking Time: 20 minutes

Serve: 2

Nutritional Value (Amount per Serving)

- Calories 408
- Fat 11.7 g
- Carbohydrates 50.8 g
- Sugar 40.7 g
- Protein 28 g
- Cholesterol 54 mg

Ingredients:

- 2 sea bass fillets
- 1/2 tsp ginger garlic paste
- 2 tbsp mirin
- 4 tbsp honey

- 1 tbsp vinegar

- 4 tbsp miso paste

- 1 tbsp olive oil

- Pepper

- Salt

Directions:

1. Preheat the air fryer to 375 F.

2. Spray fish fillets with cooking spray and season with pepper and salt.

3. Place fish fillets into the air fryer basket and cook for 15 minutes.

4. Meanwhile, heat oil in a pan over medium heat. Add miso paste, vinegar, honey, mirin, and ginger garlic paste and stir to combine.

5. Remove pan from heat. Brush fish fillets with a miso glaze.

6. Serve and enjoy.

Curried Cod Fillets

Preparation Time: 10 minutes

Cooking Time: 10 minutes

Serve: 2

Nutritional Value (Amount per Serving):

- Calories 181
- Fat 9.4 g
- Carbohydrates 4.4 g
- Sugar 3.5 g
- Protein 20.2 g
- Cholesterol 60 mg

Ingredients:

- 2 cod fillets
- 1/8 tsp smoked paprika
- 1/8 tsp curry powder
- 1/8 tsp garlic powder

- 1/2 tsp sugar
- 1/4 cup Italian dressing
- Pepper
- Salt

Directions:

1. Add fish fillets and remaining ingredients into the bowl and mix well. Cover and place in the refrigerator for 15 minutes.
2. Preheat the air fryer to 370 F.
3. Spray air fryer basket with cooking spray.
4. Place fish fillets into the air fryer basket and cook for 10 minutes.
5. Serve and enjoy.

Garlic Lemon Tilapia

Preparation Time: 10 minutes

Cooking Time: 10 minutes

Serve: 2

Nutritional Value (Amount per Serving):

- Calories 97
- Fat 1.1 g
- Carbohydrates 0.9 g
- Sugar 0.2 g
- Protein 21.2 g
- Cholesterol 55 mg

Ingredients:

- 2 tilapia fillets
- 1/2 tsp lemon pepper seasoning
- 1/2 tsp garlic powder

- Pepper
- Salt

Directions:

1. Preheat the air fryer to 360 F.

2. Spray fish fillets with cooking spray.

3. Season fish fillets with lemon pepper seasoning, garlic powder, pepper, and salt.

4. Place fish fillets into the air fryer basket and cook for 10 minutes.

5. Serve and enjoy.

Super Healthy Tilapia

Preparation Time: 10 minutes

Cooking Time: 10 minutes

Serve: 2

Nutritional Value (Amount per Serving):

- Calories 183
- Fat 6.7 g
- Carbohydrates 0.7 g
- Sugar 0.2 g
- Protein 32.2 g
- Cholesterol 85 mg

Ingredients:

- 2 tilapia fillets
- 1/4 tsp smoked paprika
- 1/2 tsp garlic powder
- 2 tsp olive oil

- Pepper
- Salt

Directions:

1. Preheat the air fryer to 390 F.

2. Brush fish fillets with oil and sprinkle with paprika, garlic powder, pepper, and salt.

3. Place fish fillets into the air fryer basket and cook for 10 minutes.

4. Serve and enjoy.

Flavorful Halibut

Preparation Time: 10 minutes

Cooking Time: 12 minutes

Serve: 2

Ingredients:

- 2 halibut fillets
- 1/2 tsp onion powder
- 1/2 tsp garlic powder
- 1/4 tsp chili powder
- Pepper
- Salt

Nutritional Value (Amount per Serving):

- Calories 324
- Fat 6.8 g
- Carbohydrates 1.2 g
- Sugar 0.4 g

- Protein 60.7 g
- Cholesterol 93 mg

Directions:

1. Spray fish fillets with cooking spray.

2. Season fish fillets with onion powder, garlic powder, chili powder, pepper, and salt.

3. Place fish fillets into the air fryer basket and cook for 12 minutes.

4. Serve and enjoy.

Crispy Crusted Halibut

Preparation Time: 10 minutes

Cooking Time: 10 minutes

Serve: 4

Nutritional Value (Amount per Serving):

- Calories 467
- Fat 7.6 g
- Carbohydrates 25.3 g
- Sugar 1.2 g
- Protein 64.2 g
- Cholesterol 93 mg

Ingredients:

- 4 halibut fillets
- 1/2 cup white wine
- 1/2 cup cornstarch
- 2 egg whites

- 1/2 cup whole-wheat breadcrumbs
- 1/2 cup pecan, crushed
- 1/2 tsp Italian seasoning
- Pepper
- Salt

Directions:

1. In a bowl, whisk together egg whites, cornstarch, and wine.

2. In a shallow dish, mix breadcrumbs, pecans, Italian seasoning, pepper, and salt.

3. Dredge the fish fillets into the egg mixture then coat with breadcrumb mixture.

4. Preheat the air fryer to 375 F.

5. Spray air fryer basket with cooking spray.

6. Place fish fillets into the air fryer basket and cook for 10 minutes.

7. Serve and enjoy.

Parmesan Halibut

Preparation Time: 10 minutes

Cooking Time: 15 minutes

Serve: 2

Nutritional Value (Amount per Serving):

- Calories 380
- Fat 13.7 g
- Carbohydrates 0.4 g
- Sugar 0.1 g
- Protein 60.6 g
- Cholesterol 93 mg

Ingredients:

- 2 halibut fillets
- 1/4 tsp garlic powder
- 1 tbsp parsley, chopped
- 1/4 cup parmesan cheese, grated

- 1/2 cup whole-wheat breadcrumbs
- 1/2 lemon juice
- 1 tbsp olive oil
- Pepper
- Salt

Directions:

1. In a shallow dish, mix breadcrumbs, cheese, parsley, garlic powder, pepper, and salt.

2. In a small bowl, mix oil and lemon juice.

3. Brush fish fillets with oil mixture and coat with breadcrumb mixture.

4. Place fish fillets into the air fryer basket and cook at 400 F for 12-15 minutes.

5. Serve and enjoy.

Garlic Herb Tilapia

Preparation Time: 10 minutes

Cooking Time: 12 minutes

Serve: 4

Nutritional Value (Amount per Serving):

- Calories 130
- Fat 4.5 g
- Carbohydrates 0 g
- Sugar 0 g
- Protein 22 g
- Cholesterol 100 mg

Ingredients:

- 4 tilapia fillets
- 1 tbsp olive oil
- 1 tbsp garlic herb seasoning

Directions:

1. Preheat the air fryer to 400 F.

2. Brush fish fillets with oil and sprinkle with seasoning.

3. Place fish fillets into the air fryer basket and cook for 12 minutes.

4. Serve and enjoy.

Crispy Catfish Fillets

Preparation Time: 10 minutes

Cooking Time: 20 minutes

Serve: 4

Nutritional Value (Amount per Serving):

- Calories 326
- Fat 13.2 g
- Carbohydrates 23.5 g
- Sugar 0.2 g
- Protein 27.4 g
- Cholesterol 75 mg

Ingredients:

- 4 catfish fillets
- 3 tsp Cajun seasoning
- 1 cup cornmeal
- Pepper
- Salt

Directions:

1. In a shallow dish, mix cornmeal, pepper, Cajun seasoning, and salt.

2. Coat fish fillets with cornmeal mixture and place into the air fryer basket and cook at 390 F for 15 minutes.

3. Turn temperature to 400 F and cook fish fillets for 5 minutes more.

4. Serve and enjoy.

Simple & Tasty Tilapia

Preparation Time: 10 minutes

Cooking Time: 5 minutes

Serve: 4

Nutritional Value (Amount per Serving):

- Calories 266
- Fat 13.1 g
- Carbohydrates 23.1 g
- Sugar 1.1 g
- Protein 13.4 g
- Cholesterol 66 mg

Ingredients:

- 1 egg, lightly beaten
- 1 tbsp old bay seasoning
- 1 cup whole-wheat breadcrumbs
- 4 tilapia fish fillets

Directions:

1. Preheat the air fryer to 400 F.

2. In a small dish, add egg and whisk well.

3. In a shallow dish, mix breadcrumbs and seasoning.

4. Dip fish fillets in egg then coat with breadcrumb mixture.

5. Place fish fillets into the air fryer basket and cook for 5 minutes.

6. Serve and enjoy.

Juicy & Tender Tilapia

Preparation Time: 10 minutes

Cooking Time: 10 minutes

Serve: 2

Ingredients:

2 tilapia fillets

1 tsp garlic, minced

2 tsp parsley, chopped

2 tsp chives, chopped

2 tsp olive oil

Pepper

Salt

Nutritional Value (Amount per Serving):

- Calories 143
- Fat 5.7 g
- Carbohydrates 0.6 g
- Sugar 0 g
- Protein 22.2 g
- Cholesterol 100 mg

Directions:

1. Preheat the air fryer to 400 F.

2. In a small bowl, mix oil, chives, parsley, garlic, pepper, and salt.

3. Brush fish fillets with oil mixture and place into the air fryer basket and cook for 10 minutes.

4. Serve and enjoy.

Lightning Source UK Ltd.
Milton Keynes UK
UKHW022011310822
408147UK00003B/349